FINISH IN

4

10 Steps to Graduating College in 4 Years

by

Miguel A. Gonzalez III

muckraker**media**

Published by:

The Muckraker Media Corp.
7324 Gaston Ave #124-349
Dallas, Texas 75214

For more information, email info@muckmedia.com or visit www.finishin4.net.

ISBN: 978-0-9851695-1-0

First edition

To my wife, with whom, I find the courage to be who I am; I thank God for you every day.

Special thanks to **Reina Santana**, your advice is always needed and always appreciated. You are the ultimate professional.

Thanks to everyone that has supported me throughout the writing process of this book. Your review, thoughts, critiques, and experiences have helped me to help so many students and I thank you!

muckraker**media**

WWW.MUCKMEDIA.COM

WHY IS THIS BOOK SO SMALL?

In life, I have always been attracted to the idea that "less is more." Shortening a sentence while still achieving its point has been a writing goal of mine. I am no martyr. I like big, huge, and impressive words like anyone else; however, I often find the sentence is diluted rather than improved. I would rather have a string of meaningful small "literary explosions" than yarns of pointless "fictional outbursts." I hope this small book achieves the goal of aiding you in your quest of graduating college in 4 years. If it does, this tiny book will have made a huge impact.

Enjoy!

Miguel

STEP 1: GET A PLAN

"By failing to prepare, you are preparing to fail."

— Benjamin Franklin

The above statement could not be truer—most students who fail to graduate college in 4 years never implemented a plan to help them achieve their graduation goal. Wishing is not planning, hoping is not planning, and crossing your fingers is not planning. Planning is planning. Always keep this important FACT in mind: Graduating college is your responsibility—NOT your parents' responsibility. If you don't graduate (or graduate on time), it's no one's fault but your own.

You should have a plan for each year of college.

Each year should have a specific goal:

- Freshman Year - *Time to discover*

- Sophomore Year - *Time to decide on a major* (if you have not done so already)

- Junior Year - *Internship time*

- Senior Year - *Time to graduate and get a job*

It's really that simple. Sure, there will be many other objectives and goals in between, but fundamentally, your goals are that simple. Let's examine the ideal 4-year plan:

Freshman year

- Get a 4.0 GPA

- Get involved with all the activities you want

- Begin dating and fall in love

- Become best friends with your roommate

Sophomore year

- Keep your 4.0 GPA

- Juggle all your activities easily

- Fall deeper in love

Junior Year

- Still have a 4.0

- Find the perfect internship

- Get pre-engaged

Senior year

- Graduate with honors

- Get engaged

- Land a great job with an enormous salary

- Live happily ever after...

By now I hope you realize the previous 4-year plan is just a dream! Maybe some students have college careers like this, but most of us live in an imperfect world where things go wrong, sometimes for no good reason. This is why you must plan.

No plan means no direction, and no direction means you have no path to hop back on when you get off course.

Finishing college in 4 years is easy IF you have a 4-year plan to meet your goal.

4 YEAR COLLEGES GRADUATE 53% OF STUDENTS IN 6 YEARS
USA Today Online 6/3/2009

The above headline is the shocking reality—most students DO NOT graduate college in 4 years. Actually, only 53% graduate in 6 years! The rest either graduate afterward or not at all.

Just because you start college does not mean you finish. Each year of college that you spend over your 4-year goal costs you:

- **Lost wages**
- **Lost experience**
- **Bigger school loans and tuition**

These are just a few of the consequences of sticking around college longer than the intended 4 years. Not only that, but financial aid does not last forever. It is based on a 4-year model. If you prolong your graduation date, you risk losing your financial aid as well.

The good news is that many things in college can be controlled.

The part you can control is the part you need to plan.
Things like:

- How many credits *you will* take per semester

- What *you will* do if you fail a class

- How *you will* pay for school if your parents can no
  longer afford your tuition

These are all situations you should think about BEFORE
they happen. This is an important principle of planning; it
should happen before, not during, and certainly not after,
the crisis occurs.

If you can learn how to plan, then you will be on the road
to success. If you can see it, you can do it.

Hang out with graduates...not dropouts.

Yes, I know. I sound like a parent, but parents are often right because they have learned from their numerous mistakes.

A very old saying is, "If you lie with dogs, you'll wake up with fleas."

No truer words have ever been said. Just in case you need an interpretation: if you hang out with losers, you will adopt loser habits. This is especially true in college. If your friends are the pot-smoking, beer-drinking students who rarely attend classes, your chances of graduating in 4 years are slim. This also goes for those in a dating relationship. If your "significant other" has little aspirations of finishing school on time or never gives it much thought, then it will only be a matter of time before their philosophy rubs off on you.

A good rule of thumb: try to find friends who are, or are headed, toward where you want to be. Hang out with the 4.0 students. It's not shameless, it's smart. Make friends with the student body president. Join an academic club, if you like. The more people you are around who are focused on achieving the same goals as you, the more likely you are to achieve yours.

Remember, all people are created equal BUT not all people use their freedom equally. So hang out with the people who take their right to an education seriously. Choose your friends wisely.

Go to orientation.

If you have already missed orientation, you will soon see why this is important. Orientation is not a useless formality and there are many important reasons for attending.

First, you might get to meet your professors, advisors, and many other individuals on your campus who will serve as important resources throughout your college career.

The great thing is that everyone will be introduced to you all at once. This will make your college transition simple and help you stay focused when you arrive. Don't be the kid at the party who walks into a room full of people you don't know. That can be lonely and frustrating!

Secondly, you have the opportunity to be reintroduced to the school. For most students, the college tour was the last time they visited the college. Orientation can give you a good sense of what the semester might be like. It won't be completely like the upcoming semester, but you will start to get a sense of the institution and the support systems in place.

Lastly, you can meet a friend or two. Sometimes you even stumble across your lifelong best friends. Again, make sure these folks are fairly academically minded. They don't need to be all about the books, but they should aspire to graduate and seek to graduate in four years, just like you. A common mistake made by incoming freshman is to latch on to the first person that says "hi" just so they know somebody. If you get to know a person and they are talking about "blowing off" orientation to go look for members of the opposite sex, guess what, that's a problem.

COLLEGE TIP:

Use a schedule organizer of some sort. Blackberry, Apple it doesn't matter as long as you begin to use it faithfully. There is NO-WAY you will survive without one.

STEP 2: UNDERSTAND THE CONCEPT OF "CREDIT"

This is very important. Without understanding the concept of a credit, you can't understand the process of graduating from college. Basically, credits are the quarters that make up the dollars in college; the paycheck is graduation.

So, what is a credit? The term credit is short for credit hour which is a unit of time.

1 credit = 60 minutes of "class time."

So if you take a 3-credit class, you will (usually) spend 180 minutes in class. Got it?

The time is the same regardless of what days your class meets or whether the class meets 3 times a week or just once. No matter what, you will be in that class for 60 minutes per credit.

Read this again if you need clarity.

Take 15 credits or more per semester.

This is critical. If you do not do this, you will fall behind right at the beginning. Many universities suggest the 15-credit benchmark because it keeps you on task to graduate in 4 years. Unfortunately, there is not much wiggle room for mishaps like failed grades. That's why it's important to have a plan.

This is the overall plan of attack:

15 credits x 8 semesters = 120 credits

120 (approximate) credits are what many students need to graduate college. Some majors require more credits than others, so be certain to confirm the precise number of credits your major requires for graduation.

However many credits you need to graduate, the equation does not change:

credits x semesters = graduation

If you can understand credits, you can see the big picture, and achieve your goal of graduating in 4 years. Remember, credits are the currency that makes graduation possible.

COLLEGE TIP:
Get a copy of your undergraduate catalog. It has all the information to enable you to graduate from your institution. It is a treasure map in college.

STEP 3: GET GUIDANCE

In college, the advisor is your guide. Just like the vacationer who wants to explore the jungle needs a tour guide, so do you. Many arrogant tourists tromping through the jungle have been devoured by lions simply because of their lack of direction and knowledge.

College can be almost as dangerous as the jungle, especially for freshman. Don't be cocky. Find your advisor and meet with them regularly.

I say "find your advisor" because in some cases it's not easy to locate them. Every college is different, so it is difficult to give an exact plan of action. However, it's typically safe to assume someone knows who your college advisor is. In any event, "Who is my advisor?" ought to be one of the first questions that you ask during orientation.

Let's just say you don't get to meet your college advisor until the second semester (or even after!). This would be highly unfortunate, because students need significant guidance their first semester. But if that's the way your school does it, you must compensate for the school's oversight.

Find a mentor or a mentoring program.

With any luck, your university has a mentoring program for incoming students. Some mentoring programs start in the summer, but many start in the fall, usually when classes begin. Mentoring is good for everyone, and it's an especially useful for a student who does not have ample guidance their first semester.

No matter what your situation, find help and get a guide.

Don't get eaten up by the lions while you tiptoe through the jungle. Get a guide and take firm steps toward your college success.

COLLEGE TIP:

Be friendly towards the secretary and office staff of your department. In truth, they are the people that make things move. So, be smart and be nice.

STEP 4: DECIDE ON A MAJOR BEFORE JUNIOR YEAR

Decide on a major as early as possible because it assures that your class credits will count toward graduation.

Every college is different, but it's safe to assume that you should have a major before the end of sophomore year (your fourth semester).

Don't over-stress about a major.

It's a known fact that many people major in subjects in college that do not become their careers.

Unless you are planning to become a nurse or another major where a specific undergraduate degree is essential, don't sweat it. My advice is to do what interests you. If you do something interesting, your grades will be better and college will be a lot more fun.

The truth is that attaining a 4-year college degree is the objective for most students. So, pick a major. Don't change your major unless you are absolutely sure your graduation status will not be impeded. And even then, think twice, especially if you want to "Finish in 4." That said, it's important to remember that attaining the best degree for you is an honorable goal. If your chosen major doesn't make you happy, change it and find something more gratifying. However, if you decide to change your major, understand the consequences: you might stay in school longer than 4 years. Make sure you weigh the pros and cons. That is part of being a true adult. Remember, whatever you decide, plan out your path ahead of time.

COLLEGE TIP:

If you're undeclared be certain to start thinking about a major soon. Your advisor is a good resource for this type of decision.

STEP 5: GO TO CLASS…AND DO YOUR WORK

This might seem obvious, but most incoming college students overlook this step. This oversight happens for many reasons. Here are a few:

Cockiness is right next to stupidity.

It never ceases to amaze me how smart people can sometimes be so dumb. I say this because students who come to college hauling a "magnificent" GPA and "breathtaking" SAT scores overrate the importance of those accomplishments and undervalue the importance of purely "hitting the books." High school might have been simple for you. College might not be. The dumb part is assuming the first semester of college will be as easy as any semester of high school. It probably will not be.

If you find out it's easy, great, but don't assume it will be. Self-confidence is good; however, cockiness is an overestimation of ability based solely on prior performance in a totally different arena. That is dumb.

Go to class.

When most new students realize they might not "have" to attend classes in college, they usually don't attend. This is a mistake. Your professor might not care if you show up to class, but it's your grade on the line. Some professors just don't take attendance, while some consider you adult enough to make your own decision. Don't begin your college career skipping classes. Just be conservative and attend them.

In addition, while you are in class, don't sleep off last night's party –pay attention. There's nothing more frustrating to a professor than listening to a student snoring in the back of the classroom. Don't just come to class; take a seat in the front row. This demonstrates to the professor that you are interested and willing to be engaged.

Many professors give points for class participation and those points can make a huge difference in your final grade. This is yet another reason to show up for class. You can lose valuable class participation points if you "play hooky."

The college syllabus is the bible of any class.

I can't emphasize this point enough—your whole semester is mapped out in your syllabus.

It's generally that simple. Most college professors will not remind you about upcoming assignments, so it's up to you to consult your syllabus. Don't be caught like a deer in the headlights when you walk into class and the teacher asks for all assignments to be placed on the desk before class begins. It doesn't feel pleasant, believe me. Consult your syllabus, do your work, and go to class.

The good news is this: if you study when you need to study, you will feel better about playing when it's time to play. This way, you can enjoy the best of both worlds.

COLLEGE TIP:

Go to professor's office hours. This shows the professor that you care about the class. This small act can pay big dividends toward your grade.

STEP 6: GET YOUR MONEY RIGHT

Money is a fundamental part of life. This is especially true in college. That does not mean you need to have a lot of money in the bank to go to college. But you do need to have a way of paying for it. That "way" might be financial aid or your parents. However you decide to pay, make sure you plan ahead. Don't take a back seat while your parents work out all the financial obligations of school. This is both lazy and immature. At the very least, you should know what's going on with the finances. In the end, it will be your education on the line if there is no way to pay the bill.

So, if you have questions, ask them. Ask until you understand. In theory, these people work for you.
I don't mean that rudely or that you should be obnoxious toward the financial aid officers, but you should leave with a thorough understanding of how the process works. That is part of their job.

So, ask many, many questions at the financial aid office. If you don't ask questions, you won't understand what is going on and you will get into trouble. Most students are passive with the financial aid process. This is the kiss of death. You will probably end up signing documents you don't understand. Even if you ask someone to paraphrase the document (if you don't plan on reading it), that's better than nothing.

I recommend you read everything meticulously and understand it fully, but whatever works and whatever helps you understand the process is what's best to do. Sometimes, receiving financial aid from the government through the school can be a very difficult process to understand and monitor. You must jump through many hoops and keep a close watch on deadlines or you could end up losing your aid and possibly lose a semester of school.

There are many rules that tie your financial aid to your GPA and credits earned. These rules are fundamental to learn. In most schools, if your GPA is under a 2.0 for an academic year (2 semesters), you will likely lose your financial aid, and the only way to get it back is to boost your GPA. This might be tricky to do, especially if you have no financial aid money to pay for school. So, how do you get your GPA up?

This is a situation that many students find themselves in and they often lose semesters or drop out completely.

So make sure you are on top of your finances, before they get on top of you.

COLLEGE TIP:

If you are going to work…try and do as little hours as possible without going bankrupt. Many students try and work too many hours and end up graduating later. Financially, this is suicide.

STEP 7: TRY NOT TO TRANSFER COLLEGES

Many students enter their freshman year with the intention of transferring to another institution. There are many reasons why they would do this. One of the most popular is that the student was not accepted to their first-choice school. Therefore, in their minds, this is a "temporary stop" until they can get into their "real college." This is understandable because we all want to fulfill our dreams and aspirations. But keep this fact in mind: **Transferring schools is one of the quickest ways to lose college credits and prolong your graduation.** This is because many universities will not take credits from other universities. And if they do, the process can be long and confusing. So, unless you have a first-class reason for transferring that cannot be worked out at your present institution, don't transfer.

That's only if you want to "Finish in 4." Some people get lucky and many of their credits transfer, but that is the exception, not the rule. Most transfer students lose credits and it can add up to a full 2 years on their graduation date. You should consider this before transferring institutions.

Obviously, this does not apply to students coming from community colleges or 2-year institutions. These schools are set up to transfer credits to other institutions, but even here you might lose credits once making the change to a 4-year school. Just to be safe, try to go to a 4-year school at the beginning of your college career. That way you can graduate without any major mishap.

I know a young woman who transferred institutions and was transformed from an incoming junior (third-year student) to an incoming sophomore (second-year student). By transferring, she lost an entire year of college instantly.

After some advice from me (and others), she decided to take some extra classes at her local community college to make up the lost credits. In her case, she was willing to sacrifice some free time to stay on schedule to graduate. If you are not willing to do the same, don't transfer schools. In any event, whatever you decide to do, be certain to weigh the risks and benefits of your decision first.

COLLEGE TIP:

If you're entering a community college investigate if the school has articulation agreements with any four year institutions. These predetermined policies will enable you to transfer into these schools without losing credits.

STEP 8: GO TO SUMMER SCHOOL

Yes, I know, everybody hates summer school. Typically, summer school is thought to be punishment for not doing your work during the school year. But that is high-school thinking.

Summer school in college can be a smart way to ensure you will graduate in 4 years because it will allow you to make up failed or missed classes. This can keep you on track when no other solution is available.

Summer classes can also be an opportunity to develop a rapport with professors, possibly within your major. This rapport will pay dividends once the semester starts and you are already familiar with the professor's teaching style.

Last, but not least, summer school can be an opportunity to meet motivated students both in and out of your major. This could be the biggest plus of all.

The good news is that most universities accept credits from each other for summer school classes. Be certain to confirm this with your college. However, it's almost certain that you can take classes at another 4-year institution close to your home or a local community college during the summer. This can help save you money, too, because most community colleges are significantly less expensive than 4-year schools.

This will also take some pressure off of you during the regular semesters because you will be taking classes in the summer that might not be available during the fall or spring semesters.

Remember that for this to work, you must plan ahead. Many universities give you several months of prior notice so you have time to plan your summer school classes. Take advantage of this and plan your summer in advance. As many universities have several sessions, you might be able to take an early or a late summer session that would allow you plenty of time for vacationing or working or both. Planning is essential. Again, the earlier you master the art of planning, the earlier you will realize your goals in college and in life.

COLLEGE TIP:

Community Colleges are great places to take summer classes. Be certain to find out if your credits will transfer back to your home school before you take a class!

STEP 9: GET READY TO GRADUATE

Finally, we get to graduation.

For a college student, graduation is what it's all about.

However, there are a few things to remember so the transition goes smoothly and you can be assured of graduating on time.

First, make sure you are on track to receiving all of your credits before graduation. There is normally someone at each university who is in charge of signing off that your graduation requirements are met.

Make sure you know who this person is and set up an appointment with them early. Don't wait until a week before graduation before tackling this issue. Often times, you can walk in the ceremony and make up your credits in the summer after your graduation. But no matter what, have a plan. Know in advance if you will be doing this. Don't assume anything. Especially not when your graduation is on the line.

Make up any incompletes or missed classes. This is the time to finally get in touch with someone in regards to the professor who retired after you took their class and received an incomplete. It might have been two years since you tried to tackle this problem but it still can be resolved. Contacting the chair of the department is a good start. Hopefully you know who this is. If not, find out quickly.

Sewing up all of the loose ends is what senior year is all about. Focus, focus, and focus some more. That is the name of the game during your last two semesters. You are at the finish line...run Forrest, run...the end is in sight.

This is the time to pay those delinquent parking tickets and library book fees. Make sure you plan to have a zero balance before you leave. Many schools will hold your degree until you pay. This can hurt you if you need proof of graduation for a job that's awaiting you after college.

It is these small details that can bring your college journey to a halt. So just pay attention to the small stuff and it will help you avoid big problems later.

COLLEGE TIP:

Find the person who will do your final sign off on your graduation. Most times they are found in the registration office.

STEP 10: HAVE FUN!

Yes, I saved the fun for last, but I highly recommend having fun in college.

I also guarantee that if you follow my previous nine steps, you will have extra fun in college because you will be organized and diligent with your most important priority: graduating!

Joining organizations, making friends, playing sports, and enjoying your college experience are important because your undergraduate years only come once.

So you must enjoy it!

On the other hand, sorry to say, many students' primary focus when they enter college is fun. And since this book is in essence a "cautionary tale," I must leave you with this final observation on the illusions and consequences of too much fun and not enough work.

One of my favorite movies of all time is National Lampoon's Animal House. This movie is the ultimate depiction of college life as being ALL about fun. I cannot remember a single scene where any of the main characters attended classes. Growing up, I thought this was funny. I still do when I watch the movie now as an adult.

But one thing I notice as an adult that I failed to spot when I was younger is that none of the fraternity guys who put enjoyment before their studies left Faber College with a degree.

In other words, at the end of the movie most of those guys were NOT college graduates.

Don't let that be your movie ending. Have fun, but also make sure that graduating from college in four years is your number one priority.

Good luck, and God Bless!

COLLEGE TIP:

Join a campus organization. Fraternities, Sororities, Honor Societies, Band, and Campus Clubs are all wonderful ways of staying busy in college while learning valuable leadership skills.

GLOSSARY OF IMPORTANT COLLEGE TERMS:

Academic Probation - Students are placed on academic probation when they are in danger of being dismissed from the school because of low grades. Many colleges put students on probation if their GPA is below a 2.0.

Accreditation - If a school is accredited, it means that the school has met the accrediting organization's competency requirements.

Admissions - The department designed to go through each application and decide who to admit for the following year.

Advisor - A designated professor in the department that the student is in who is assigned to help them along their four years, as well as assist them in choosing their classes.

Associate's Degree - Students who complete a 2-year program receive an associate's degree.

Bachelor's Degree - Students who complete a 4- or 5-year program receive a bachelor's degree.

Credit Hour - As a general rule, the number of credit hours assigned to a course also indicates the number of hours the class meets per week. A 3-hour course, for example, usually meets 3 hours a week. Lab classes are the exception; they usually meet for longer time periods.

Drop/Add - Students who want to drop or add a course must complete the required form(s) before the drop/add deadline(s).

Elective - All students must take a certain number of required courses. Elective courses are those that students choose, or "elect," to take.

Major - This is the academic area that a student studies in-depth.

Prerequisite - When students must take one course before they are allowed to take another, the first course is a prerequisite. Math 101, for example, might be a prerequisite for Math 102.

Quarter/Semester - Colleges on quarters divide their year into three academic terms of about 12 weeks each. Colleges on semesters divide their school year into 2 equal periods.

Registration - Before the beginning of each term, students must pay their fees and sign up (register) for classes.

Room and Board - Refers to the amount of money that students who live on campus must pay for housing (room) and meals (board).

Transcript - A copy of a student's official academic record that lists all courses taken and all grades and credits earned. Transcripts can be obtained from the registrar's office.

Transfer of Credits - Students who attend an accredited college usually find that their credits will transfer. The college to which the student is transferring decides which credits they will accept.

Tuition - The amount of money charged for academic instruction.

Undeclared - A student who has not yet decided on a field of study has an undeclared major.

Undergraduate - A student who has not yet received a bachelor's degree, but is in the process.

GLOSSARY OF COLLEGE DEPARTMENTS:

Academic Affairs - Usually responsible for all academic issues at a university

Advancement - Raises money for the university and is often coupled with Alumni Affairs; sometimes awards scholarships

Counseling Office - Available for students who might need to talk about personal problems and/or school related stresses

Disability Services - Support for those who have a documented disability

Diversity/Multicultural Affairs - Discrimination complaints and programming support for minorities and other protected groups

Enrollment Services - Includes registrar, bursar and admissions

Facilities - Responsible for the landscaping and maintenance of buildings on campus

Health - All on-campus medical needs

Orientation - Responsible for helping incoming students become familiar with the campus

Residence Life and Housing - Deals with all dorm and housing issues

Student Activities - Coordinates all social programs on campus

Student Affairs - Responsible for most student-centered programs and initiatives

Student Recreation Complex (SRC) - Most often a building on campus that students can utilize for exercise, activities, and recreational sports

ABOUT THE AUTHOR:

Miguel Gonzalez is a higher education professional who has held leadership positions in Student Recruitment, Student Retention, and Veteran Affairs. Miguel's extensive background has made him the perfect person to write such a book. With less than 50% of American college students finishing college within 6 years, the odds are against students graduating in 4 years, or at all. *Finish In 4* is a culmination of his insights into the higher education system and what all students can do to navigate that system. Whether a student is in their freshman year of college or senior year in high school, this book is a must-have. He has developed guidance that is simple, direct, and written for the student!

For more information about Miguel Gonzalez or to have Miguel speak at your institution, please contact info@muckmedia.com or call (214) 884-8588.

LEARN MORE:

For more information about Finish In 4 or

other projects, please find us on Facebook

www.facebook.com/10stepstograd

& Twitter https://twitter.com/finishin4